Chicago and Northwestern Railway Company

Memorial of the Chicago and Northwestern and Chicago, Milwaukee and St. Paul Railway Companies

Chicago and Northwestern Railway Company

Memorial of the Chicago and Northwestern and Chicago, Milwaukee and St. Paul Railway Companies

ISBN/EAN: 9783744696838

Printed in Europe, USA, Canada, Australia, Japan

Cover: Foto ©ninafisch / pixelio.de

More available books at **www.hansebooks.com**

MEMORIAL

OF THE

CHICAGO & NORTH W

AND

Chicago, Milwaukee

RAILWAY COM

TO THE

SENATE AND

(
OF T

STATE

TO THE HONORABLE THE

SENATE AND ASSEMBLY

OF THE

STATE OF WISCONSIN.

The Memorial of the Chicago & Northwestern and Chicago, Milwaukee & St. Paul Railway Companies respectfully represents:

During the controversy growing out of the demand for cheaper transportation, it has frequently been affirmed that no injustice was meditated against the railway interests of the State. Yet it is possible that, with the best intentions, serious mistakes may be committed. Under a misconception of the facts, great injury may be done. Complaints which, at first, seem grievous, would often, if understood, lose their force; but, remaining unexplained, they give rise to burdensome inflictions.

Knowing this, your memorialists are encouraged to lay before your honorable body a statement of the principles upon which railway operations can alone be successfully conducted. If rightly considered, it should serve to remove many false impressions now engraven on the popular mind. To these errors the outcry against corporations is largely due. Especially is this true of

DISCRIMINATION.

The trouble is, no distinction is made between just and unjust discrimination. Believing distance to be the controlling element in framing a tariff, the public fail to see why the same or a greater rate should be charged for a shorter haul. Consequently, they demand pro rata tariffs.

This aspect of the question is not a new one. It has provoked many conflicts in Europe—legislative and judicial. Upon nine separate occasions the justice of the principle was discussed before Select Committees of the British Parliament. Eight times they sanctioned the practice and rejected the equal mileage plan, and once they came to no decision.

The public still being dissatisfied and clamorous for equal mileage rates, a Select Committee of both Houses of Parliament was appointed, in 1872, to thoroughly investigate the matter. Their sessions extended over a period of five months, during which witnesses representing every interest affected by railways were carefully examined, and the objections and advantages of the proposition freely discussed. Passing in admirable review the various complaints and remedies which American Legislatures annually throw out as novelties, they conclude that

"EQUAL MILEAGE RATES ARE INEXPEDIENT,"*

and give the following reasons why such proposition "is impracticable:"

"(*a*) It would prevent railway companies from lowering their fares and rates so as to compete with traffic by sea, by canal, or by a shorter or otherwise cheaper railway, and would thus deprive the public of the benefit of competition and the company of a legitimate source of profit.

"(*b*) It would prevent railway companies from making perfectly fair arrangements for carrying at a lower rate than usual goods brought in large and constant quantities, or for carrying for long distances at a lower rate than for short distances.

"(*c*) It would compel a company to carry for the same rate over a line which has been very expensive in construction, or which, from gradients or otherwise, is very expensive in working, at the same rate at which it carries over other lines."†

THE INJUSTICE OF MAKING DISTANCE A CONTROLLING PRINCIPLE

may be illustrated: Madison is much nearer Milwaukee than is Prairie du Chien, and would, apparently, be entitled to much lower rates. Yet its business costs a mere trifle less. A train of empty cars leaves Milwaukee, the requisite number are dropped at Madison and other way stations, and, at Prairie du Chien the return trip is commenced. The locomotive starts with the capacity to haul a full train, but may not have more than ten or twelve cars until it approaches Milwaukee. The cars left at Madison are there picked up. Meantime they have been motionless, and cars earn money only when in motion. Having had to provide force enough to move a full train, the Prairie du Chien freight is thus carried to Milwaukee nearly as cheaply to the company as that from way stations.

The Lake Superior trade is a case in point. The supplies for that

* Report Railway Companies Amalgamation, p. 11.
† Ib. p. xxxii.

market are taken there by water and by rail; but the exports, being mineral, are all carried away by lake. There is no return freight for the loaded cars sent north. When Menomonee, Oconto or Green Bay are reached, coming south, lumber is offered for shipment. Vessels are ready to take it at a low rate. The railroad company must accept their rate or pass on with the empty cars. Now it is evident that, no expense being added, the rate derived, though small, is so much gain, and, by helping to meet current expenses, enables the company to do its regular business cheaper than it otherwise could. Yet, if forced to do *all* business at those rates, the company could not pay expenses and interest upon its bonds.

Experience demonstrates that

RAILROADS MUST BE RUN ON COMMERCIAL PRINCIPLES.

The rates from competing points must be the same over all routes, irrespective of their length, if they would share in the carrying trade. The shortest route fixes the rate, and the longer roads must accept that rate or forego the business. This natural law of trade the British Parliament recognized by enacting that, "if the competing routes are not unreasonably circuitous or inconvenient, the same gross rate shall be charged."

The justice of such provision is manifest. Were pro rata tariffs enforced, the shorter route would be assured *a monopoly of the business.*

In lamenting the high rates for local traffic, the

ADVANTAGES CONFERRED BY THROUGH LINES

are overlooked. They provide constant avenues and markets for the business along the line. Heretofore this business was at a stand-still for months, excepting such portion as could be done by teaming. The surrounding community have, therefore, reaped the advantage of the difference between railroad charges and the cost of teaming, and between a business of twelve months instead of a few months in the year.

When the States of Maryland, Virginia, Pennsylvania and New York entered upon the construction of their canals, a ton of freight could not be carried over an ordinary highway for less than ten cents a mile, even when the highway was in the best condition; while over the country roads, new, as many in this State are, with rocky hills and soft, deep soil in the bottom lands, the cost averaged 20 cents a mile, whereas the Milwaukee & St. Paul and Northwestern Companies, last year, carried their whole tonnage at an average of $2\frac{86}{100}$ cents per ton per mile.

Were it not that repeated efforts are made to enforce uniform tariffs, it would seem unnecessary to show that it

COSTS MORE TO DO LOCAL THAN THROUGH BUSINESS.

The cars in local trains rarely run as full as in through trains. Through cars can be loaded to their full capacity, while local freight, having to be distributed along the line, cannot be compactly loaded, as it must be so placed that it can be most expeditiously unloaded. The experience of some managers is, that, of the same class of freight, only six tons of local freight can be averaged in a car, while ten tons can be carried in through cars.

Mr. Stewart, Secretary of the London and Northwestern Railway Company, testified before a Parliamentary Committee that the average weight of freight placed in English cars capable of carrying five tons, does not exceed 1¾ tons. And the fact that railway companies are obliged to run more passenger cars than are necessary to accommodate the traveling public, he illustrated by stating that on two fair average days, 4,483 passengers were ticketed from Euston Square Station, while the coaches provided contained 13,512 seats. This disproportion was largely owing to the company's sending through cars on to branch lines. The effect of this was further shown in the selection of 15 trains bound to London, on which coaches carrying only 179 through passengers contained 1,274 seats.* When the preponderance of dead weight carried is so great in a country having 420 inhabitants to the square mile, its disproportion in this State, with less than twenty persons to the square mile, can well be imagined.

But the main difference is in the lesser number of cars hauled. Through trains can be loaded to their full capacity and be so forwarded the entire length of the line; while local trains start with a few cars, pick up others on the route, and drop off some; consequently, the average number in the train differs. It is believed more money can be made at 2c. per ton per mile on long business than at 3c. per mile for local.

New business can be done cheaper than is old business because the latter is that for which the road was built, and is, therefore, chargeable with the expense of operation. Many large expenditures are not affected by the amount of business, such as maintenance of permanent way, stations and cars, damages by fire and flood, and other expenses which probably aggregate one-third of the whole.

---

* Royal Commission, p. lxxvii.

ACTION OF OTHER STATES.

When this question came before the New York legislature, in 1860, it was shown that nearly one-third of the expenses of railway management were not affected by the increase of business.

Before the same Committee Mr. Minot testified that the approximate cost of way freight on the New York and Erie Railway averaged 50 per cent. more than the through.

And when the question came before a Special Committee of the Senate of Alabama, in 1873, the chairman, in his report, gave this practical illustration: "Ordinarily it requires 24 hours to load a car and 24 hours to unload it. The average speed of a freight train is ten miles an hour. A car carries ten tons of freight. Suppose the rate charged to be 2c. per mile; if the car is to be moved ten miles, it would require 49 hours, and it would earn for the company $2.00, that is, 96c. per day.

"If this same car were to be moved 1,000 miles, it would require 148 hours, and, at the same rate of freight, would earn $32.50 per day.

"Now if to this calculation be also added the loss to the company from the locomotive continuing its trip with a train of less weight than it had capacity to draw, and also the additional expense to the company of station houses and station agents and employes at different points to accommodate the local business, but which are of no use for through business, it becomes palpable the transportation of freight over short distances justifies a discrimination and a charge of a much higher rate per mile of distance than is necessary when the transportation is over long distances."

REASONS FOR UNEQUAL RATES.

It requires as much time and labor to receive, handle and bill the goods and collect the charges when the freight is destined five miles as it does if consigned 500 miles. And it is not possible to name a rate per mile that would be deemed fair and equitable for five miles which would also be applicable to 500 miles. If the short rate thus ascertained were applied to long distances, many necessaries—such as grain—could not be moved, because the freight would exceed the value of the article shipped.

Usually, local freight is not unloaded as promptly as is through freight. Now a car is worth, say $10 per day in the busy season; therefore, when one is delayed four days, the company loses $40, while the charges for the short haul might not exceed $10. The running expenses of cars in motion are merely nominal compared with those incident to delay at stations and on side tracks.

If local rates were obliged to be made to correspond with through rates, the companies would be forced out of the through traffic.

An illustration is found in the grain traffic of the Upper Mississippi. Powerful efforts have been made to divert it down the river to St. Louis and New Orleans, and latterly, to have it seek the Atlantic via Duluth. To defeat these attempts the produce had, sometimes, to be carried across Wisconsin at a loss. Were the companies forced to lower their local rates to these competitive figures they could not do so and live. They would, then, be obliged to forego that trade and quietly submit to see it pass by Wisconsin and reach the sea by an unfettered route.

If the

EXPERIENCE OF OTHER COUNTRIES

would be accepted as authority, results sufficiently plain to guide the legislature could be plentifully adduced. The bitterest complaints in England have always been that, by reason of unequal rates, certain districts received advantages which better enabled them to compete for business than others. The respective rights of the railways and the public were defined in the general railroad law* by the declaration "it is expedient that the company should "be enabled to vary the tolls upon the railway so as to accommodate "them to the circumstances of the traffic;" and the company was authorized "from time to time to alter or vary the tolls, either upon "the whole or upon any particular portion of the railway as they "shall see fit."

And in the year 1867, a Royal Commission, after investigating the subject in all its bearings, reported that "Inequality of charge "in respect of distance, besides being a necessary consequence of "* * competition, is an essential element in the carrying trade; "that is to say, the principle which governs a railway company in "fixing the rate is that of creating a traffic by charging such a sum "for conveyance as will induce the produce of one district to compete with that of another in a common market.

"The power of granting special rates thus permits a development "of trade which would not otherwise exist, and it is abundantly evident that a large portion of the trade of the country at the present time has been created by and is continued on the faith of

---

*The Railway Clauses Consolidation Act.

"special rates." And they conclusively add: "The conditions "under which such rates are granted are so numerous that no spe-"cial law could be framed to regulate them." *

Granting that such latitude would confer great power on railway managers, it is clearly

THEIR INTEREST TO DEVELOP THE TRADE

of their respective districts. For example, in 1864, during a temporary stoppage of the coal supply, the North Staffordshire Railway Company of England, which was dependent upon the prosperity of the pottery trade, carried coal from the Derbyshire coal mines to the Staffordshire potteries at a rate of freight barely in excess of working expenses. Had they not done so the pottery trade would have come to a stand-still, and the railway company would have suffered great loss.†

By the exercise of such discretion railway companies encourage the location of manufactures and greatly aid in placing them on a permanent basis.

UNEQUAL RATES SANCTIONED BY THE COURTS.

The right of a company to charge unequal rates has been affirmed by the English Courts. In the case of Ransome v. Eastern Counties Ry., 8 C. B. (N. S.) 709, the Court of Common Pleas held that a company may charge different rates for carriage where the expenses thereof are different; and that, as the expense of starting a train is the same for a great or small distance, this may fairly be taken into account and justify an inequality in the rates of carriage between different places.

And in Nicholson v. Great Western Ry. Co., 4 C. B. (N. S.) 366, the same Court held that it is not "giving an undue or unreasonable preference to carry goods for one person at a lower rate than the Company does for another when it does so in consideration of a guaranty of large quantities and full train loads at regular periods, provided the real object of the company is to obtain thereby a greater remunerative profit by the diminished cost of carriage, although the effect may be to exclude from the lower rate those persons who cannot give such guaranty." The Court further say that a company may make special contracts securing advantages to individual shippers where it clearly appears that, in making such agreements, the company has only the interests of the proprietors in view.

* Royal Commission on Railways, p. xlvii.
† Ib., p. xlvii.

In regard to varying passenger rates on different parts of the same railway, the Court held, in Caterham Railway Co. *in. re.* 1 C. B. (N. S.) 410, that higher charges on one branch line than on another do not *per se* constitute an undue advantage.

RELATIVE COST OF MOVING FREIGHT.

The cost of movement varies with the circumstances of the several roads. One may have an abundance of coal along its line, while others may have to transport their fuel many miles to the depots of supply.

Another may have a comparatively level, straight road-bed, over which an ordinary locomotive can haul forty or fifty cars, containing ten tons each; while a rival road, or another portion of the same line, may have such heavy grades and sharp curves that the same power cannot draw one-half the load. Such is the case on the Tunnel Section of the Northwestern railway, in Monroe county. There, two of the most powerful engines are required to draw one-half the load an ordinary locomotive can haul upon a comparatively level line. In that event, the cost per mile on the heavy part is four times that on the level line. For every grade of 20 feet to the mile the work required to overcome it is estimated as equal to that expended on two miles of level road.

Presuming on the perfect condition of the road and engine, a locomotive that will move ninety loaded cars on a level grade, will haul only fifty-six cars on a grade of ten feet to the mile; and, on a grade of twenty feet, it will haul forty cars—showing a difference between a grade of twenty feet and a level grade of two and one-quarter to one. On a thirty feet grade the same engine will haul thirty-one cars; on a forty feet grade, twenty-five cars; on a fifty feet grade, twenty-one cars, and on a sixty feet grade, eighteen cars.*

COST INCREASED BY UNUSED CAPACITY.

The cost is further increased by the amount of unused capacity and the dead weight carried. Suppose two roads have cost the same, the tariff prescribed for one may be unprofitable to the other on account of lack of business. Therefore, in making comparisons between different lines, justice requires an examination into the amount of business done. Thus, as shown in Exhibit A, the Pennsylvania railroad last year carried 9,211,231 tons of freight, or 11,124 tons per mile of road operated; while the Chicago & Northwestern

* Report of Col. J. H. Simson to the Secretary of the Interior, Sept. 16, 1865.

carried, during the same period, 3,591,090 tons, or 2,411 tons per mile, and the Milwaukee & St. Paul Railway, 1,752,706 tons during the year, or 1,252 tons to the mile of road. That is, the Northwestern, with its 1,489 miles of road, did only 38 per cent., and the Milwaukee & St. Paul, with 1,400 miles, 19 per cent. of the business done by the Pennsylvania upon less than 900 miles of road. Similar deductions are shown by comparisons with the freight movement on all Eastern trunk lines.

The result is, that, in consequence of the vast amount of business done by those roads, even though taken at an average rate of $1\frac{1}{2}$ cents per ton per mile, against $2\frac{22}{100}$ cents received by the Northwestern, and $2\frac{50}{100}$ cents by the St. Paul Company, the gross earnings per mile of the Boston & Albany railroad exceed those of the Northwestern Company nearly four times and those of the St. Paul Company five times, while its *net earnings* are much larger, per mile, than are the gross earnings of the latter Company.

The differences are still more striking in the net results of the New York Central and Pennsylvania, the former being seven times and the latter six times greater than those of the Milwaukee & St. Paul railway for the same period.

Comparisons with Ohio and New England Roads show similar results. [See Exhibits B and C]. The Cinn., Ham. & Dayton railroad carried, during the year 1873, a total of 9,927 tons per mile, and the Cleveland & Pittsburgh railroad 10,611 tons per mile; and, despite an average lower rate per ton per mile, the *net* earnings per mile of three of these roads exceed the *gross* earnings per mile of Wisconsin roads; while all of them show much larger gross results per mile.

CURRENT OF TRADE IN ONE DIRECTION.

Trade currents are mainly in one direction. Four-fifths of the loaded cars hauled eastward over the Pennsylvania railroad, during 1873, were returned empty; and 72 per cent. of the Erie Railway traffic for the same year was eastward bound. During the month of August, 1873, the Chicago & Alton railroad received 7,585 loaded cars at Chicago, but, in order to do so, had to send out 5,394 empty cars.

On the Milwaukee & St. Paul railway the disproportion was still greater—1,358,745 tons being carried eastward, and 432,759 tons westward. That is, the west-bound freight was only 31 per cent. of the east-bound. The same general results are observable on the Chicago & Northwestern, the Lake Shore, and the Michigan Central railroads, as shown in Exhibit A.

Were the movement of freight more equalized, the cost of transportation would be largely reduced. Yet the irregularity of business demands as large an equipment as though it were constant.

The earning traffic being mainly in one direction, the cars, in order to earn at all, must be returned to be reloaded. If returned empty, the freight carried must make up the loss. Even a slight income, earned by the return cars, would help to meet the general expenses; therefore, the best rate obtainable under the circumstances, would seem to be reasonable.

In the case of four fifths of the traffic, when a shipper at Ripon, Sparta, or any station distant from the lake, calls for cars in which to ship wheat to Milwaukee, the companies have to send empty cars, so that it is equivalent to making a double trip in order to secure freight for one trip.

COST OF RUNNING FAST.

Foreign railway companies recognize that speed is the essence of expense by making lower rates for passengers and freights carried by slow trains. The estimate of experts is, that expenses increase as the square of the velocity; but the ratio is even greater, that is, if the speed of the engine is doubled, the cost of the wear and tear of the road is more than quadrupled.

Moving, loaded cars represent

THE EARNING EQUIPMENT OF A ROAD,

and upon their use largely depends the relation between profit and loss. Each road having the financial ability, possesses the number of cars experience shows to be necessary for its operations at the busiest season. But the income per car, at that time, would not be a fair criterion of the business of the road, nor of the average value of the entire equipment.

This can be illustrated by the operations of the Chicago & Northwestern railway for the six months ending Nov. 30, 1874. The car equipment comprised 6,628 cars, exclusive of ore cars. Of this number 215 made no mileage, leaving 6,413 to make all the movements. The actual car mileage was 30,662,291 miles, equivalent to 306,662,-910 ton mileage, while the *actual* ton mileage was but 212,275,311, or 69 per cent. of the mileage the cars were forced to make on account of the irregular distribution of the freight.

The actual freight mileage capacity of the cars, allowing ample time for loading and unloading, and for the disability of a liberal number, is about 144,000,000 car mileage, or 1,440,000,000 ton mileage, while the actual ton mileage performed was 212,275,311, which shows that the actual car mileage was only fifteen per cent. of the car mileage the equipment required by the fluctuating business is capable of doing.

And this per centage is further reduced by the fact that, of the actual car mileage made, about 75 per cent. only was paying ton mileage, which shows that the total tonnage of the Chicago & North-western system is but 11 per cent. of the capacity of the rolling stock the Company is obliged to keep; that is, were the freight constant, regular and in car loads, 739 cars would do the same business which now requires 6,628 cars.

Keeping in view this

GREAT DISPROPORTION

between what Western railroads are able to do and what is given them to do, let us contrast the operations of leading Eastern lines. The fairest way is to take the tonnage carried one mile.

During the year 1873, the Milwaukee & St. Paul Railway, operating 1399 miles of road, carried 257,638,532 tons one mile, or, 184,159 tons per mile of road, at an average rate of $2\frac{50}{100}$ cents per ton per mile; while the New York Central, with 858 miles of road, carried 1,244,650,063 tons one mile, or, 1,452,972 tons per mile of road, at an average rate of $1\frac{57}{100}$ cents per ton per mile. Thus, the movement per mile of road on the Milwaukee & St. Paul was only 12 per cent. that of the New York Central.

Similar results are deducible from comparisons with other Eastern roads, as shown in Exhibits A and C, the figures in which are taken from their own published reports and late State documents.

Taking these standards, it must be apparent that the Wisconsin companies, having costly roads which are not worked up to one-fifth of their capacity, their tariffs must necessarily, in order to meet fixed and current expenses, tax the tonnage that is moved much more, per ton, than would be the case were the capacity of the roads attained or even approximated.

COST DECREASES AS BUSINESS INCREASES.

The expense of transportation decreases as the volume of freight increases. To forward a single letter from the Atlantic to the Pacific coast, by special messenger, would cost several hundred dollars. Deposited in the Government mails, three cents pays for its transportation. This cheap service is possible because, simultaneously, a like service is performed for thousands of other patrons.

In establishing the route, the Government provided all the appliances for the service, and the increased cost of conveying one hundred or one thousand additional letters in each mail compared with the larger revenue yielded, is scarcely appreciable.

Freight transportation is subject to the same law. Facilities for doing a large, constant business are provided; therefore the cost per ton when a vast tonnage is moved must be inconsiderable compared with the cost when but a small amount is carried.

The impression is general that Western roads charge much higher rates than do Eastern roads. Often it is said that it costs as much to move produce to the lakes as it does thence to the sea. This arises from the fact that *Western local rates are compared with Eastern through rates.* Compare the local tariffs of the respective roads and a different result is shown. To aid in this investigation several comparative tables have been prepared and appended hereto as exhibits. They present

MATTER FOR DEEP REFLECTION.

The classes enumerated in the Potter law as D, E, F, G, H, I, J, were selected, and the distance rates prescribed therein are contrasted with the published rates for like services on leading Eastern and Western roads.

A glance at the lumber rates will be instructive—[Exhibit D.] For a distance of 200 miles the Pennsylvania Road charge $61 per car load; the Boston & Albany, $48; Vermont Central, $46; Erie, $37; Great Western, Michigan Central, and Illinois Central, each $38; Lake Shore & Michigan Southern, $35; Indianapolis, Cincinnati & Lafayette, $56; and Hannibal & St. Joe, $65 per car load. For the same service the Potter law allows $25 per car. The roads named do a large lumber business. Three of them start from the chief lumber market; and another—the Vermont Central, whose rate is $46—runs through Burlington, the fourth largest lumber point in the country.

The comparative statement of grain rates is scarcely less suggestive. [Exhibit E.] For a distance of 225 miles the rates per 100 lbs. are: on the Vermont Central, 31c.; Boston & Albany, 30c.; Erie, 27c.; Pennsylvania, 36c.; Pittsburgh & Fort Wayne, 32c.; St. Louis, Kansas City & Northern, 34c; and Chicago, Burlington & Quincy, 36c. The Potter law allows 22½c. for the service.

On Flour—[Exhibit F.] the Potter law rate for 200 miles is: 44c. per bbl., while the Vermont Central charge 80c.; the Boston

& Albany, 60c.: Pennsylvania, 72c.; Erie, 50c.; Fort Wayne, 67c.; Great Western of Canada, 52c.; Hannibal & St. Joe, 50c.; St. Louis, Kansas City & Northern, 67c.; and C., B. & Q., 70c. per barrel.

On Live Stock—[Exhibit G]—the Potter law allows $25 per car load for 100 miles; the Boston & Albany charge $36; the Vermont Central, $34; the Fort Wayne, $45; the Hannibal & St. Joe, $39; Louisville & Nashville, $45; and the C., B. & Q., $47.

But the comparative rates on Agricultural Implements, Furniture and Wagons—[Exhibit H] are most remarkable. In some cases the difference exceeds 100 per cent. Take the rates for 150 miles. The Potter law presumes that $29 per car load is a fair rate. The Vermont Central, Indianapolis, Cincinnati & Lafayette, Hannibal & St. Joe, and Chicago, Burlington & Quincy—running through rich manufacturing and agricultural districts—charge more than double the Wisconsin rate, while the Great Western of Canada charge $49; the Fort Wayne, $48; Michigan Central, $42; and the St. Louis, Kansas City & Northern Road, $55 per car load.

The rates on Salt, Cement and Lime—[Exhibit I]—and on Coal, Brick, Sand, Stone, etc.,—[Exhibit J]—are not less instructive. In fact all the tables will repay careful perusal.

THE SHOWING WOULD HAVE BEEN STILL WORSE

had the distance rates on the roads named, for say, 40, 70, 90, 120 and 140 miles, been taken instead of for each successive 25 miles, as the Potter law rates do not vary for that distance until the next 25 miles are reached. The rates given are taken from the latest published tariffs of the several roads, many of the figures being filled in by the General Freight Agents of the respective companies. Their study should dispel the illusion that Eastern lines carry for a mere bagatelle compared with the rates enforced on Western roads.

It should also be remembered that a great difference exists between the business done by Western roads and that given to the trunk lines. The railways which radiate from Lake Michigan and run like lattice-work throughout the West, gather up business, and, centering at Chicago, pour it by train loads on to the tracks of the through lines to the East. The latter have simply to forward it. It is this fortunate condition which gives the New York Central Railroad sixteen miles of freight cars daily! The Western roads are feeders; the Eastern lines are receivers. The latter are saved the expense of picking up this business by driblets. It comes to them in volumes. Trains follow each other in quick succession, and their constant movement ensures economy.

This desirable condition, and the efforts to obtain it, impel the companies to form connections with what are commonly termed

UNPROFITABLE OUTSIDE LINES.

Complaint is made that the people of Wisconsin and Illinois have to pay the cost of supporting certain Iowa and Minnesota lines. A glance at the facts will show how much truth is in the charge. The Galena Division of the Chicago & Northwestern Railway furnishes an apt illustration. Thirty miles west of Chicago the double track line diverges, one running northwest through Belvidere and Rockford to Freeport; the other continuing westward via Dixon and Sterling to the Mississippi. The Freeport line has no through connection. Its business is entirely local. The Dixon Air Line connects with several Iowa roads and from them receives a large traffic. Both lines run through a rich, populous country—fitly termed the garden of Illinois. Mark the different results. The gross earnings of the Freeport Line for the year 1873 were $8,201.36 per mile; while those of the Dixon Air Line were $20,556.76 per mile, the through business contributed by the "outside lines" being the sole occasion of the difference.

Without such contributions from connecting lines, it is not apparent how the Madison Extension of the Northwestern Railway could pick up local business enough to pay its operating expenses.

To make the investigation more thorough, comparisons have been made with

FOREIGN RAILWAY TARIFFS.

The lines selected are among the leading roads of Great Britain. One of them operates 1,539 miles, and the mileage of two others aggregate nearly 2,400 miles. [Exhibit R.] Their charges are taken from the returns made by them to a Royal Commission appointed for that purpose. For 100 miles the rate on Flour per barrel [Exhibit K] is, on the Midland Railway, 36c.; North Eastern, 36c.; Great Eastern, 30c.; London, Brighton & South Coast, 30c.; and Glasgow & South Western, 40c. The Potter law allows 28c. For longer distances the disproportion is still greater.

Comparisons on grain rates show similar results. For 150 miles the Potter law allows 18c. per 100 lbs.; while the Midland Railway charge 27c.; the N. Eastern, 27c.; Great Eastern, 22c.; London, Brighton & South Coast Railway, 22 cents; and Glasgow & South Western Railway, 30c.

The rates on Flour and Grain are especially fair comparisons, because it is notorious that, in order to foster manufactures by securing cheap labor, the British Government has always endeavored to keep low the price of breadstuffs.

Upon Salt and Cement—[Exhibit L] the differences are even greater. For 150 miles the Potter law allows 35c. per barrel. The Midland Railway charge 84c.; the North Eastern, 53c.; Midland Great Western of Ireland, 63c.; and the Glasgow & South Western of Scotland, 84c. per barrel.

Upon Agricultural Implements and Wagons—[Exhibit M] the rates are 100 per cent. higher. The rates on these articles are fixed by the Railway Clearing House, and are the same for all roads belonging to that association. For 100 miles the Potter law rate is $23 per car load. On the English roads it is $43.75. For 125 miles, Potter law rate, $26; English rate, $53.75; and for 150 miles, Potter law rate, $29; English rate, $63.75.

Appended to the Report recently made to Congress by Senator Windom, of Minnesota, Chairman of the Select Committee on Transportation-Routes to the Seaboard, is a statement of through rates for freight on English railways, which confirms the differences herein shown. For example,* the English rate on Flour, per bbl., for 150 and 300 miles, is 44 cents and 72 cents respectively. The Potter law allows 36 cents and 43 cents for the same distances. On Lumber, the car-load rate for 150 miles is $44, against $21 named in the Potter law. Upon Salt, Cement, and Lime, per bbl., the English rate for 150 miles is 85 cents; Potter law rate, 56 cents per bbl.; while upon Agricultural Implements, Furniture and Wagons, per car-load, the English rate is $96, against $29 allowed by the Potter law.

To dissipate any doubt regarding the correctness of the comparisons, the tariffs and reports † from which they were taken will be laid before your Honorable body, if desired.§

Nor is it desired the exceptionally low rates charged by the Atlantic & Great Western Railway should be overlooked. They are and have been such that the company—controlled by Mr.

---

* Transportation Routes to Seaboard; Appendix, p. 223.

† Appendices to Evidence—Royal Commission on Railways.

§ In all these foreign tariffs, the charges are stated at a given rate per ton per mile. In arriving at the comparisons, the premium on gold is made to offset the difference between the English and the American ton.

McHenry, the English low rate advocate—has failed to meet its obligations and the road is now in the hands of a Receiver; which warrants the belief that a similar fate awaits any corporation that hazards the experiment of doing business at a loss.

The comparative differences are still more remarkable in view of

THE RELATIVE COST OF OPERATING ROADS.

The cost per mile run on the Milwaukee & St. Paul Railway, last year, was $1.39. On the Cleveland & Pittsburgh Road it was 54c. per train mile; on the Philadelphia & Reading, 61c.; on the Pennsylvania Road, 95c.; and on the Michigan Central, $1.22. Upon 28 Massachusetts roads it averaged $1.28, and upon all the roads in Great Britain, in 1872, it averaged 66c. per train mile. When it is remembered that the miles run upon each of the roads named extend well up into the millions, it will be manifest that the aggregate cost of operating roads in the West, with their lighter business, is vastly greater than in the East.

This is aggravated by the

INCREASED COST OF FUEL.

Pennsylvania and Ohio railways procure their coal supply at about $1.50 per ton; and the Illinois companies which traverse mining regions obtain their supply at an average of $1.80 per ton. Wisconsin companies are not so fortunate. They are obliged to pay $4 or $5 per ton for an inferior, soft coal.

Practically, the cheapness of fuel levels the Alleghany mountains. The heavy grades on the Pennsylvania Raiload simply demand additional power, and the steam created by their abundant fuel lifts the vast tonnage over the mountains at a less cost than Wisconsin and Minnesota companies can operate in the open country.

The mass of the people being much exercised about

PASSENGER RATES,

comparisons with the practice of other States and countries will be of service. Where population is dense, the earnings from passengers form nearly one-half the gross receipts. This result is seen in England—[Exhibit N]—where the passenger receipts, in 1872, were 41 per cent. of the gross earnings. On the Chicago & North Western Railway, last year, they were 23 per cent., and on the Milwaukee & St. Paul Railway, 20 per cent. Yet, as shown in Exhibit O, the first-class fare on all the English roads named exceeds 5c. per mile, and, in two cases, exceeds 6c.; while the second-class fare averages 4c. per mile, and only third-class accommodations are given for 2c. per mile.

True, the conditions of passenger travel are not precisely analagous. Society in England is divided into three classes—upper, middle and lower—and the companies felt obliged to make the distinctions. For a time third-class passengers were not carried on express trains, but were restricted to the single slow train Parliament required each company to run daily.* Since the change, receipts from third-class passengers have increased until, in 1872, they exceeded the combined receipts from first and second-class travel. Similar experiments in this country have failed. The proud consciousness that one man is as good as another, and is, therefore, entitled to the same accommodations, will not allow any one to put up with third-class fare.

The popular theory that

REDUCED PASSENGER RATES

will produce a greater net revenue by inducing a proportionate increase of travel, is true only upon conditions not yet found in the West. To most men, the time occupied away from their business, hotel bills and other expenses incident to travel, have a greater bearing upon their movements than a few cents difference in the railway fare. In a rich, populous country, adjacent to a large city, where the time employed as well as the attendant expenses are less, the travel will certainly be larger at low rates than at higher rates, though by no means in proportion to the decrease.

The English railway companies having been mulcted in heavy damages for injuries to passengers traveling at the lowest rates, Parliament, on requiring a certain company to run cheap trains to and from London, limited the liability of the company in respect of passengers by those trains†—a consideration the justice of which is beyond dispute.

A CONTRAST.

In Germany, third class passengers are huddled together in rough, open cars, and are often obliged to stand in close order during their transit. In this country a passenger receives, for second class English rates, room enough, in parlor coaches, for a bed on which he can lie down and sleep to his journey's end.

* The earnings derived from Parliamentary trains are exempt from taxation, and the trains are not required to be run faster than 12 miles an hour, whereas express trains average over 40 miles an hour.—Ry. Co's. Amal, p. xvi.

† Report Royal Commission, p. lxxvii.

The rates in Prussia are: by express trains,—first class, $4\frac{1}{2}$ cents per mile; by ordinary trains,—first class, $3\frac{45}{100}$ cents; second class, $2\frac{67}{100}$ cents; and third class, $1\frac{76}{100}$ cents.

In Austria the rates are: by express trains,—first class, 5 cents per mile; by ordinary trains,—first class, $4\frac{11}{100}$ cents; second class, $3\frac{10}{100}$ cents, and third class, $2\frac{06}{100}$ cents.

In addition to these rates,* for all baggage in excess of 50 lbs. there is a charge of 17 cents to 25 cents per ton per mile.

England has an area of 50,922 square miles, and contains over 21,400,000 inhabitants, or 420 persons to the square mile. The chief railway traffic, as in Belgium, France and Germany, is connected with mining, iron works and manufacturing. These industries occasion the most travel,† while this State is almost wholly agricultural, causing but little movement among the people.

Frequent reference is made to the

NEW YORK CENTRAL RATE OF TWO CENTS PER MILE.

No other road is so fortunately located. From Suspension Bridge and Buffalo to New York city it traverses a country rich in agricultural and industrial resources, and dotted as thickly with populous cities as there are farm houses along many Wisconsin lines This unequaled advantage enables that Company to profitably run 50 passenger trains daily, while two, each way, amply accommodate the limited travel in this State. Nor should the still more significant fact be overlooked that the *net* earnings from passengers alone on the New York Central, during 1873, were $2,035 per mile—a much larger revenue per mile than the net results *from all sources* on the Milwaukee & St. Paul railway for the last fiscal year.

The solution is found in the far larger number of passengers per mile carried by lines in other States than is possible in Wisconsin with the present sparse population of the State.

During the year 1873, the Milwaukee & St. Paul railway carried 967,754 passengers, or 692 persons to the mile of road operated, while the Boston & Albany railway carried 20,417 passengers per mile; the Boston & Lowell, 30,537; the Connecticut River road, 20,077; the Eastern of Mass., 21,277; the New York & New Haven, 25,542; the United roads of New Jersey, 28,790, and the Boston & Providence as many as 56,690 passengers to the mile of road.

---

* Report Royal Commission, p. lvii.

† Mass. Commissioners' 2d Annual Report.

During the same period, the Chicago & Northwestern railway carried 1,869 passengers per mile. [See Exhibit S.]

An examination of the

RATES ON OHIO RAILROADS

shows an average, for the shortest distances, of 5 cents per mile; and, for less than 30 miles, 4 cents per mile, while the average for long distances is $3\frac{1}{2}$ cents per mile. [Exhibit P]. Comparisons with Ohio are better because the passenger earnings per mile more nearly approach the proportion on Wisconsin lines. Nine different tariffs were prescribed by the Legislature of that State for the railroads, but these proving inoperative, the companies are now allowed the utmost freedom.

THE CHEAP RATES IN BELGIUM

being often cited, we have taken pains to look into that system. The Belgium railways were commenced by the State after the Revolution of 1830, at a time when private enterprise was unequal to the task of constructing them. The necessary money was borrowed on the principle that it should be gradually redeemed by periodical payments charged upon the net revenue, and, *until they became profitable*, the funds necessary to reduce the debt were advanced from the State Treasury. From 1837 to 1851, inclusive, the expenditures largely exceeded the receipts, varying from £239,530 sterling, in 1841, on 211 miles of railway, to £12,915, in 1851, on 387 miles of road. Up to 1867, the 435 miles of State railway had cost $106,968 per mile. No reduction in rates was attempted until after the net profits, in 1854, on the 535 miles, had amounted to about $830,000.*

Regarding passengers, there are three classes of travel and two kinds of service—by ordinary trains and by express trains. Upon the latter the rates are 20 per cent. higher. The usual rates per mile upon express trains are: 1st class, $3\frac{41}{100}$ cents; 2d class, $2\frac{55}{100}$ cents; 3d class, $1\frac{62}{100}$ cents.

These rates, *with an extra charge* of 20 cents per ton per mile for all baggage other than that a passenger can carry in his hand or stow under the seat without inconvenience, are allowed in

THE MOST THICKLY PEOPLED COUNTRY IN THE WORLD,

where express trains are frequent and where labor is distressingly cheap. With an area of only 11,374 square miles, Belgium, in

---

* Railways (Ireland) Commission, page 8.

1872, had 5,087,105 inhabitants, or 447 persons to the square mile; and 2,900 persons to each mile of railway.

Wisconsin has an area of 56,000 square miles, a population of 1,054,670, and 2,531 miles of railway, or 18 inhabitants to the square mile, and 416 persons to each mile of railway.

In view of this exhibit, it is especially deserving of notice that the Belgian railways charge, for Live Stock, per car load, $21 for a distance of 50 miles, and $27.81 for 100 miles, while the Potter law limits us to $17 for 50 miles, and $23 for 100 miles.

On Agricultural Implements, the Belgian rate, by slow trains, for 30 miles, is $11.30 per car load. The Potter law rate is $11. For 60 miles the Belgian rate is $21.00, while the Potter law allows but $14. For longer distances the ratio of increase shows still greater differences, and these extend to Flour, Grain, and the other articles enumerated in the Potter law, as may be seen by reference to the Blue Book * from which the figures are taken.

IN FRANCE

there is practically no competition among the railways. As far back as 1852, the entire railway system passed into the control of six companies, each of which was allotted a specified territory. Their efforts to construct secondary lines proving unsuccessful, the State came to their relief and guaranteed the interest on their obligations for fifty years, together with an excess to be applied in creating a sinking fund. Up to January 1st, 1865, the State had aided the six companies, in money and works, to the amount of 1,293,502,509 francs.†

In view of the aid given and the immunity from competition assured the French railways, it may be worth while to look at a few of their charges.

From Calais to Paris, a distance of one hundred and eighty-five miles, the through rates are: first-class, $4\frac{1}{2}$ cents per mile; second-class, $3\frac{15}{100}$ cents; and third-class, $2\frac{29}{100}$ cents per mile. On the Paris, Lyon & Marseilles Railway, from Lyon to Marseilles, 540 miles, the rates are: first-class, $4\frac{15}{100}$ cents; second-class, $3\frac{12}{100}$ cents; and third-class, $2\frac{28}{100}$ cents per mile.

In regard to freight a few cases will suffice.§ "From Paris to Amiens—eighty-five miles—the rate on grain is 13 cents per 100 pounds; and on flour, 27 cents per barrel. The Potter law rates are 12 cents per 100 pounds, and 24 cents per barrel.

---

* Railways (Ireland) Commission, p. 22 and p. 74 App. to Ev.
† Appendices to Ev. Royal Com., p. 285.
§ App. to Ev. Royal Commission, p. 239.

For a car load of furniture the same road charges $39 for eighty-five miles. The Potter law allows $20.

On lumber, the French railways charge $19.20 per car load for fifty miles, and $26.20 for seventy-five miles. The Potter law allows $13 for fifty miles and $15 for seventy-five miles. The corresponding English rates are much higher than the French rates.*

COST OF RAILROADS.

When a road is graded, laid with iron and declared open for business, the popular impression is that the work is finished; whereas it is only fairly begun. Considerable ballasting and surfacing are required and a great many warehouses, elevators and station buildings must be provided, together with a large amount of rolling stock and numerous other facilities, before much business can be safely done. Cuts have to be widened, sidings put in, bridges and culverts strengthened, fences built, renewals made, and many other improvements which add to the cost of construction. And, as no railroad is or can be made profitable without it starts from a large city, the right of way within such corporate limits and the ground needed for sidings, warehouses and depots, costs enormously; but, every part of the road being benefited by these facilities, the cost is apportioned over the whole road.

Those who demur to the statement that any Wisconsin road could, possibly, cost more than $30,000 per mile, may find it instructive to look at the statement shown in Exhibit Q. In New York, the average cost of eight roads is, $76,493 per mile; in Pennsylvania, $105,761; in Ohio, $70,350; and in New England, $71,673.

In Belgium, the 535 miles of State railway cost $106,968 per mile;† in Germany, the 3,775 miles of State and private railway had, up to 1863, cost $92,446 per mile, and paid an average dividend of $7\frac{42}{100}$ per cent.; in Austria, the State railways up to 1863, had cost an average of $96,680 per mile, and paid an average of $7\frac{31}{100}$ per cent. dividend; in France the 9,014 miles of railway up to the year 1867 had cost £319,200,000 sterling, or $194,860 of our currency, per mile; and in Great Britain, where the matter of land damages is most expensively illustrated, the 15,813 miles of railway had, up to 1872, cost an average of $180,000 gold, per mile,§ averaged, that year, $4\frac{2}{4}$ per cent. dividend upon the total capital, and yielded a net profit of $8,110 gold per mile of road operated.

* Royal Commission, p. lxxi, and App. E. D. p. 327.
† Rvs. (Irel.) Commission, p. 7.
§ Railway Returns, England and Wales, Scotland and Ireland, p. iv.

These statements may revive the platitudes about

WATERED STOCK AND ORIGINAL COST.

For many years the stockholders in Wisconsin railways have been obliged to go without dividends, the surplus earnings being expended in permanent improvements which have greatly added to the value of their property. And it would seem as fair that this surplus should be capitalized, in accordance with law, as it is for successful business men to capitalize their profits. The men who, fifteen or twenty years ago, invested their money in Chicago or Milwaukee city property instead of in the local railways, have seen their money increase one hundred per cent., and the non-dividend paying railways have been the greatest element in making the property valuable. Are these men willing to accept a return on their property based on what it originally cost or upon what it is now worth? The mere fact that one portion of a railway was purchased at a low price is no more a reason why the public should be given its service at a proportionately low rate than that a house bought at a mortgage sale should be rented by the purchaser at less than it is actually worth. Equally great has been the advance in the value of Wisconsin farms. And what element has so contributed to this increase as the building and operation of railroads?

REDUCTION OF RATES.

The plea for compulsive laws rests on the mistaken belief that railroad companies would not otherwise reduce the rates of transportation. The error of this assumption and the fact that charges have diminished with the progress of time, are shown in the following statement of the average earnings per ton per mile for the years named on the Milwaukee & St. Paul, Chicago & Northwestern, Michigan Central, Chicago, Burlington & Quincy, Lake Shore & Michigan Southern, and Chicago, Rock Island & Pacific Railroads:

	C. M. & St. P. Ry.	C. & N. W. Ry.	M. C. R. R.	C. B. & Q. Ry.	L. S. & M. S. Ry.	C. R. I & P. R. R.
1868........	$3\frac{49}{100}$	$3\frac{13}{100}$	$2\frac{45}{100}$	$3\frac{20}{100}$	$2\frac{43}{100}$	....
1869........	$3\frac{10}{100}$	*	$2\frac{9}{100}$	$3\frac{1}{100}$	$2\frac{34}{100}$	$2\frac{74}{100}$
1870........	$2\frac{82}{100}$	$3\frac{9}{100}$	$1\frac{98}{100}$	$2\frac{77}{100}$	$1\frac{50}{100}$	$2\frac{64}{100}$
1871........	$2\frac{54}{100}$	$2\frac{87}{100}$	$1\frac{81}{100}$	$2\frac{31}{100}$	$1\frac{30}{100}$	$2\frac{49}{100}$
1872........	$2\frac{43}{100}$	$2\frac{51}{100}$	$1\frac{56}{100}$	$2\frac{19}{100}$	$1\frac{37}{100}$	$2\frac{29}{100}$
1873........	$2\frac{60}{100}$	$2\frac{35}{100}$	$1\frac{57}{100}$	$2\frac{18}{100}$	$1\frac{33}{100}$	$2\frac{07}{100}$

* Records for 1869 destroyed in Chicago Fire.

Railway managers endeavor so to arrange their rates that, with economy, the net receipts will yield

A REASONABLE RETURN.

The investment is a permanent one. It cannot be removed at will like a merchant's stock, nor can it be sold readily as a farm. It is the possession of an association simply because an individual cannot own or buy a railroad.

A proper schedule of rates depends upon various considerations, chief of which is the cost of transportation. There must, necessarily, be a margin between the cost of the service rendered and the compensation paid for it. A knowledge of the cost can be gained only after a careful study of the working expenses of each particular road for a period long enough to comprehend its varying circumstances and arrive at a fair average.

From whatever source the means to construct the railroads were derived, current expenses and accruing interest must be met. If the revenue obtained is not sufficient to meet the obligations, the public must endure the discomfort and inconvenience of poor roads; for unprofitable railways cannot respond to the requirements of the public. Undeniably, then, the interests of all parties are best served when enterprises of public utility are established on a remunerative basis.

Wisconsin companies have not reached that prosperous condition. The depressing fact is, that no railroad company having its lines wholly in this State is now able to pay operating expenses and the interest upon its bonded debt.

Your memorialists believe that the facts herein presented show that, in no State in the Union, and in no foreign country whose railway charges have come to their knowledge, are the rates so low as those established by the law in this State. Nevertheless, they are aware that some members of your honorable body, as well as many of the people you represent, may believe, that, owing to the happy condition of this State in reference to the subject of transportation, they are entitled to lower rates than are enjoyed by any other people, and still do ample justice to the railway companies.

It is difficult, within the limits necessarily imposed upon them in this communication, to furnish all the evidence fairly entitled to consideration on such a question. But your attention is respectfully called to some facts, showing what their earnings, net and gross, were in this State when the companies were controlled only by the laws of business and of competition in fixing their rates.

It is confidently submitted that no member of the legislature, and no citizen of the State will deny the right of capital invested in railways to a fair return. The Chicago & Northwestern Railway Company operate in this State 565$\frac{23}{100}$ miles of railway, consisting of the following lines:

1. From Sharon, Wis., to the Michigan State Line,	220.80	miles.
2. From Beloit to the west end of the Winona Bridge, at Winona, Minn., ...	205.60	"
3. From Milwaukee to Fond du Lac, . .	62.63	"
4. From Kenosha to the State Line, east of Harvard, Ill., ...	27.50	"
5. From the Illinois State Line to Geneva Lake,	8.70	"
6. From Milwaukee south to the Illinois State Line, ...	40.00	"

Of the second line, that portion from Madison to Trempeleau Junction, 30 miles south of Winona, is subject to a first mortgage, drawing seven per cent. gold interest, amounting to $3,150,000. From Trempeleau Junction to the west end of the Winona Bridge, it is subject to a first mortgage of $1,000,000, drawing ten per cent. currency interest. The line from Beloit to Madison is subject to a first mortgage, bearing seven per cent. currency interest, amounting to $306,000.

The third line is subject to a first mortgage of $3,500,000, drawing seven per cent. gold interest.

Of the line first named, 23 miles,—from Oshkosh to Appleton—are subject to a first mortgage of $147,000. From Appleton to Fort Howard, the line is subject to a first mortgage of $282,000. The two last mortgages are at seven per cent. currency interest. From Fort Howard to Menomonee the line is subject to a first mortgage amounting to $1,172,340, drawing gold interest.

All the lines named are covered by two mortgages, being part of the consolidated mortgages of the company, of which the proper proportion applicable to the Wisconsin lines amount to $3,618,925.50, drawing seven per cent. interest, partly gold and partly currency.

The line from Sharon to Oshkosh is subject to three mortgages, in connection with the rest of the line from Sharon south to Chicago, of which the proportion applicable to the Wisconsin portion of the line amounts to $3,561,786, drawing seven per cent. currency interest.

The sixth line before named is subject to two mortgages, of

which the amount applicable to the State of Wisconsin is $874,822.80, drawing interest at seven per cent.

The amount of money required each year to pay the interest on that part of these mortgages which lie in the State of Wisconsin, is $1,350,135.35.

The line from Madison to Trempeleau Junction, before named, has cost, besides the amount realized from the sale of the mortgage bonds above named, $2,559,135.38, and is represented only by the stock, common and preferred, of the Chicago & Northwestern Railway Company. The line from Trempeleau Junction to the west end of Winona Bridge has cost, besides the proceeds of the mortgage, $376,774.06, which is likewise represented only in the stock of the Chicago & Northwestern Railway Company.

The amount realized from these mortgages was used only in the construction of all the lines named, and in so far finishing them as to make it possible to use them. A very large proportion of the rolling stock required to do their business is only represented by the stock of the company.

To arrive at the amount of earnings of the Wisconsin lines for any one year it is necessary to partially estimate them, as, in the accounts of the company, the earnings of the lines are not separated by the boundaries of the State. The principle upon which the earnings are determined, for the purposes of this statement, is to take the earnings of the whole line in Illinois and Wisconsin and credit the Wisconsin portion of the lines with that proportion of the whole earnings that the miles in Wisconsin bear to the whole number of miles constituting the aggregate of the lines in the different States.

Upon that basis the gross earnings of the Wisconsin roads for the year ending December 31st, 1873, the last calendar year for which the accounts are now made up, amounts to $3,190,523.64.

The same principle is applied in ascertaining the operating expenses of the Wisconsin lines for the period named. The expenses of the through lines included in both States are divided among the States in proportion to the number of miles operated in each. The terminal expenses in Chicago on the business of the through lines are apportioned to the State of Wisconsin upon the same basis. This shows the operating expenses of the line in Wisconsin for the same year to have been $2,163,578.21, which left as the net proceeds of the business of that State applicable to the payment of interest upon its bonded debt and dividends upon its stock, the sum of $1,026,945.43.

The account would stand thus:

Gross earnings, ...	$3,190,523.64
Operating expenses, ...	2,163,578.21
Amount applicable to interest, . . .	1,026,945.43
Amount required to pay interest, . .	1,350,135.35
Deficit, ...	$323,189.92

The capital stock of the Chicago & Northwestern Railway Company applicable to the lines in Wisconsin, ascertained upon the principle that was applied in determining the earnings and operating expenses, amounts to $15,097,902.24.

It is not possible within the limits allowed us, to show how and for what this stock was created. For our present purpose it would seem sufficient to show that it represents nearly three millions of dollars actually expended in the construction of lines within the State during the last five years, and all the rolling stock in use upon the new lines the company has built since 1864, and to show that not a dollar of that large investment has ever received any return whatever. The year 1873 was selected for the reason that, during that year the company had uncontrolled power over its rates, and because a fair average business was done, and it is the last calendar year for which the accounts are made up.

Your memorialists, therefore, respectfully submit that a law reducing rates already inadequate—not only destroying all hope of dividends but lessening their ability to pay their interest—has no feature which can commend itself to the candid judgment of honest men.

Your memorialists further represent that, were it not for extending the limits of this communication — already too long — the results of the operations of the Milwaukee & St. Paul Railway would be given, which statement would also show that the arbitrary reduction of their previous rates has been an act of injustice.

EFFECT OF THE POTTER LAW.

The actual loss to the Milwaukee & St. Paul Railway Company, occasioned by conforming to the rates prescribed in the Potter law, for the months of October, November and December last, was, in receipts from passengers, $53,313.82; and in receipts from freight, $66,726.27; total, $120,040.09.

The revenue derived by the Chicago & Northwestern Railway Company from passengers in Wisconsin during the months of October and November, 1874, were 24 per cent. less than would have been received had the fares been computed at the rates in force prior to October 1st; and the earnings from freight affected by the operation of the law were 26 per cent. less than would have been received had the rates in force prior to October last been maintained.*

INJUSTICE OF THE LAW.

Your memorialists submit that the facts herein stated show the legislation of 1874 has worked great injustice to them. They believe it has also inflicted great injury upon the best interests of the State. If associated capital in one class of enterprises can be deprived of all return by an act of the legislature, so can capital invested in all other corporate or associated enterprises. Capital has been quick to draw this deduction. Your memorialists confidently appeal to the testimony of all citizens of the State in any way interested in such enterprises in proof of the assertion that the credit of both private and municipal corporations has been greatly impaired by this legislation. Individual credits have suffered scarcely less. It could not be otherwise. Transportation is a commodity, and is sold, as personal services are sold. Railroad companies furnish the best, and are, therefore, the largest sellers. The people of the State are purchasers. The same people make the laws. If they fix the price of transportation by law, then the purchasers of one commodity in the State alone fix its price. No reasonable man can believe that business could long be done on such a basis. If the people can fix the price of one commodity, they can of all that are furnished by capital associated in corporations. No business man could be found to invest his money when it is to be managed by those who have no interest except to reduce his earnings. No man will place his capital where men not of his choosing must manage it.

Let it not be forgotten that Wisconsin will, if its growth be not materially checked, need, in the near future, more railroads. It has

---

* See Report made by C. & N. W. Ry. Co. to Railroad Commissioners.

now less than many of its sister States, having but one mile of railway to twenty-one square miles of territory, while

New York	has one	mile to	9.1	square	miles of	territory.
Pennsylvania	"	"	8.4	"	"	"
Ohio	"	"	9.4	"	"	"
Indiana	"	"	9.1	"	"	"
Illinois	"	"	8.4	"	"	"
Michigan	"	"	17.0	"	"	"
Iowa	"	"	15.7	"	"	"
Massachusetts	"	"	4.4	"	"	"
Connecticut	"	"	5.4	"	"	"

Wisconsin needs immense development of its mining, manufacturing and agricultural resources. In older states and foreign countries, capital is cheap. Wise legislation, maintaining unbroken the public faith, and guaranteeing protection and fair returns, will bring that capital here. Legislation upon opposite principles will repel it.

Believing that the interests of the railroads and the people are identical; that the law. of 1874 has been prejudicial to both, and that the interests of all will be best promoted by its abrogation, your memorialists respectfully pray that its provisions fixing arbitrary rates of fare and freight may be repealed.

All of which is respectfully submitted,

ALBERT KEEP,
President, Chicago & Northwestern Railway Company.

ALEXANDER MITCHELL,
President, Chicago, Milwaukee & St. Paul Railway Company.

EXHIBITS.

EXHIBIT "A."

Comparative Statement of Freight Moved, Rate per Ton, Revenue, Etc., with the Trunk Lines.

Name of Railroad.	No. of miles operated.	Tons of Freight Carried during 1873.	Tons of Freight Carried one mile during 1873.	Direction Carried.		Per Centage of Eastward to whole traffic.	Earnings per Ton per mile.	Gross Earnings per mile	Net Earnings per mile.	Per centage of Passr. to gross earnings.
				Eastward.	Westward.		Cents.			
Chicago, Mil. & St. Paul......	**1399**	**1,752,706**	**257,638,532**	**1,358,745**	**432,759**	**77**	**2.50**	**$6,536.00**	**$1,752.36**	**20**
New York Central.............	858	5,522,724	1,246,650,063	3,989,198	1,533,526	72	1.57	33,947 37	13,383.29	24
Erie..........................	959	6,312,702	1,032,986,809	4,579,062	1,732,640	72	1.45	20,868.20	6,664.38	18
Pennsylvania..................	828	9,211,231	1,384,831,970	6,716,302	2,854,929	72	1.41	30,055.56	11,407.85	17
Lake Shore & Mich. Southern..	1180	5,511,918	1,053,927,189	3,546,009	1,965,909	73	1.33	16,824.00	4,891.00	23
Michigan Central..............	285	1,593,954	313,401,088	1,171,689	422,267	70	1.29	21,819.00	7,405.05	30
Pitts., Ft. Wayne & Chicago....	500	2,292,644	488,628,211	1,257,987	1,034,657	52	1.44	19,831.24	8,311.36	25
Boston & Albany............	283	2,884,520	317,670,752	2,133,766	750,754	73	2.19	36,521.66	8,337.02	30
Chicago & Northwestern.....	**1489**	**3,591,090**	**461,412,080**	**2,396,030**	**1,175,060**	**67**	**2.22**	**9,638.49**	**3,408.78**	**23**

EXHIBIT "B."

Comparative Statement of Tonnage Moved, Rate per Ton, Revenue, Etc., with Ohio Roads.

NAME OF RAILROAD.	Number of miles operated.	Tons of Freight carried during 1873.	Tons of Freight carried one mile during 1873.	Gross Earnings per mile.	Net Earnings per mile.	Freight Rate per ton per mile.	Cost of Road per mile.	Stock and Debt per mile.	Average am'nt rec'd for each ton.	Per cent. of Expenses to Earnings.
						Cents.				
Chicago, Mil. & St. Paul,	**1399**	**1,752,706**	**257,638,532**	**$6,536.00**	**$1,752.36**	**2.50**	**$37,480.00**	**$38,080.00**	**$3.66**	**72.00**
Ohio & Mississippi...........	393	927,258	143,436,311	9,553.23	2,903.58	1.80	89,844.38	89,844.38	2.79	69 60
Dayton & Michigan..........	142	339,997	33,316,253	7,453.60	2,081.54	2.01	48,469.67	48,391.52	1.98	72.07
Cincinnati, Ham. & Dayton...	59	585,704	20,922,033	19,389.80	5,973.80	2.78	93,932.38	106,736.64	.98	69.19
Cleveland & Pittsburgh.......	199	2,111,708	161,117,129	16,398.97	8,246.31	1.82	78,743.92	78,634.08	1.38	49.71
Clev.,Col.,Cinn. & Indianapolis	391	1,574,608	279,427,987	12,412.19	3,743.42	1.33	42,769.14	48,227.45	2.36	69.80
Pitts., Ft. Wayne & Chicago...	503	2,365,846	488,628,211	19,831.24	8,311.36	1.44	58,013.09	76,455.68	2.97	58.09
Pittsburgh, Cinn. & St. Louis..	978	3,408,147	511,562,313	10,080.80	1,649.42	1.35	95,241 15	94.807.41	2.03	83.64
Toledo, Wabash & Western...	933	1,374,392	292,505.267	9,503.69	2,113.84	1.49	55,905.77	58,117.12	3.16	77.86
Chicago & Northwestern,...	**1489**	**3,591,090**	**461,412,030**	**9,638.49**	**3,408.78**	**2.22**	**58,058.14**	**57,802.00**	**2.86**	**64.00**

EXHIBIT "C."

Comparative Statement of Tonnage, Rate per Ton and Revenue with New England Lines During 1873.

Name of Road.	Number of miles operated.	Tons of Freight Carried During Year 1873.	Tons of Freight carried one mile during 1873.	Gross Earnings per mile.	Net Earnings per mile.	Rate per ton per mile.	Per cent. of expenses to earnings.	Cost of Road per mile.	Stock and Debt per mile.
						Cents.			
Chicago, Mil. & St. Paul Ry....	**1399**	**1,752,706**	**$257,638,532**	**$6,536.00**	**$1,752.36**	**2.50**	**72.**	**$37,480.00**	**$38,080.00**
Boston & Albany..............	283	2,884.520	317,670,752	36,521.66	8,337.02	2.19	77.38	87,636.70	105,048.01
Boston & Providence..........	66	827,575	21,350,543	27,400.12	6,441.49	3.91	76.49	63,118.64	81,042.32
Old Colony...................	256	625,251	16,790,178	9,251.08	2,770.90	4.32	70.	35,337.51	39,789.58
New York & New Haven........	141	8,95,985	38,891,498	24,549.53	9,643.98	3.05	61.50	88,887.82	109,540.63
Chicago & North Western Ry..	**1489**	**3,591,090**	**461,412,030**	**9,638.49**	**3,408.78**	**2.32**	**64.**	**58,058.14**	**57,082.00**

EXHIBIT "D."

Comparative Statement of Lumber Rates.

Rates on Lumber per Car Load.	Potter Law Rates.	Trunk Lines.						New England.				Western & Southern Roads.				
		Pennsylvania Road.	Erie Railway.	Lake Shore & Michigan Southern Railway.	Michigan Central Railroad.	Great Western Railway.	Atlantic & Great Western Railway	Vermont Central Railroad.	Boston & Albany Railroad.	New York & New Haven Railroad.	Connecticut River Railroad.	Louisville & Nashville Railroad.	Illinois Central Railroad.	Indianapolis, Cincinnati & Lafayette Railroad.	St. Louis, Kansas City & Northern Railroad.	Hannibal & St. Joe Railroad.
For 25 miles,	**$ 8.00**	$ 9.20	$ 15.50	$ 12.00	$ 14.00	$ 14.00	$ 7.00	$ 12 00	$ 14.00	$ 22.00	$ 12.50	$ 10.00	$ 18.00	$ 13.00	$ 22.00	$ 23.00
" 50 "	**13.00**	17.00	19.00	15.00	14.00	17.00	12.00	16.00	20.00	26.00	20 00	16.00	23.00	21.00	32.00	33.00
" 75 "	**15.00**	24.00	22.00	19.00	18.00	22.00	14.00	22.00	24.00	28.00	26.00	20.00	27.00	27.00	38.00	43.00
" 100 "	**17.00**	31.20	25.00	22.00	26.00	26.00	17.00	26.00	28.00	40.00	31.00	25.00	30.40	32.00	43.00	49.00
" 125 "	**19.00**	39.00	28.50	25.00	28.00	29.00	19.50	32 00	34.00	44 00	36.00	32.00	32.00	37.00	48.00	54.00
" 150 "	**21.00**	46.80	31.00	27.00	30.00	31.00	22.50	36.00	38 00	50.00	40.00	35.00	34.95	43.00	50.00	59.00
" 175 "	**23.00**	54.60	34.00	32.00	34.00	36.00	24.50	42.00	44.00	......	......	40.00	37.40	48.00	53.00	64.00
" 200 "	**25.00**	61.00	37.50	35.00	38.00	38.00	27.00	46.00	48.00	......	......	......	38.00	56.00	55.00	65.00
" 225 "	**27.00**	67.60	40.00	39.00	40.00	39.00	29.50	50.50	......	......	......	......	39.40	62.00	58.00	65.00
" 250 "	**29.00**	72.00	47.50	42.00	40.00	42.00	32.00	53.50	......	......	......	......	40.40	68.00	60.00	......
" 275 "	**31.00**	72.00	50.00	......	......	46.00	35.00	58.00	......	......	......	......	41.40	73.00	60.00	......
" 300 "	**33.00**	72.00	50.50	......	......	48.00	37.00	61.00	......	......	......	......	42.80	......	60.00	......
" 325 "	**35 00**	72.00	53.00	......	......	......	39.00	65.00	......	......	......	......	46.60	......	......	......
" 350 "	**37.00**	72.00	62.00	......	......	......	40.00	67.00	......	......	......	......	49.60	......	......	......
" 375 "	**39.00**	72.00	62.00	......	......	......	41.00	69.00	......	......	......	......	52.60	......	......	......
" 400 "	**41.00**	72.00	64.50	......	......	......	......	71.00	......	......	......	......	55.20	......	......	......
" 425 "	**43.00**	72.00	......	......	......	......	......	75.00	......	......	......	......	56.80	......	......	......
" 450 "	**45.00**	72.00	......	......	......	......	......	77.00	......	......	......	......	58.00	......	......	......

EXHIBIT "E."

Comparative Statement of Grain Rates.

Grain in Car Loads per 100 pounds.	Potter Law Rates.	N. Eng. Lines.		Trunk Lines to the East.							Western and Southern Lines.				
		Vermont Central.	Boston & Albany.	Erie Railway.	Pennsylvania.	Pitts., Ft. W. & Chi.	Lake Shore & Michigan Southern.	Michigan Central.	Atlantic & Great Western Road.	Great Western of Canada.	Chicago, Burlington & Quincy.	Indianap. Cincinnati & Lafayette.	Hannibal & St. Joe.	St. Louis, Kansas City & Northern.	Louisville&Nashville.
	Cents.	Cents.	Cents.	Cents.	Cents.	Cents.	Cents.	Cents.	Cents.	Cents.	Cents.	Cents.	Cents.	Cents.	Cents.
For 25 miles.....	**6**	8	8	8	8	7	7	7	4½	8	10	8	13	13	11
50 "	**10**	11	12	11	13	9	9	9	7	11	15	12	17	18	17
75 "	**12**	14	14	13	17	14	12	12	9	14	20	14	19	23	22
100 "	**14**	18	18	16	24	18	14	15	12	16	23	17	21	28	25
125 "	**16**	20	21	18	29	20	16	17	13	20	26	19	22	30	25
150 "	**18**	23	23	20	33	24	18	18	14	22	28	22	22	32	27
175 "	**20**	25	27	22	36	27	20	19	15	24	31	24	23	33	30
200 "	**22**	27	27	25	36	30	22	20	17	25	33	27	23	33	30
225 "	**22½**	31	30	27	36	32	24	22	18	26	36	29	..	34	..
250 "	**23**	33	..	30	36	34	25	24	19	27	38	32	..	35	..
275 "	**23½**	35	..	33	36	35	..	25	21	28	41	35	..	35	..
300 "	**24**	37	..	35	36	37	..	..	22	28	43	..	..	35	..
325 "	**24½**	39	..	38	36	38	..	..	23	..	..	..	..	..	..
350 "	**25**	40	..	40	..	39	..	..	24	..	..	..	..	..	..
375 "	**25½**	41	..	42	..	41	..	..	26	..	..	..	..	..	..
400 "	**26**	42	..	45	..	44	..	..	..	..	..	..	..	..	..

EXHIBIT "F."

Statement of Comparative Rates on Flour.

Rates on Flour per Bbl.	Potter Law Rates.	N. Eng. Lines.		Trunk Lines.						Western and Southern Roads.				
		Vermont Central.	Boston & Albany.	Pennsylvania.	Erie Railway.	P., Ft. W. & C. Ry.	Great Western Ry.	Canada Southern Railway.	Atlantic & Great Western Ry.	Louisville & Nashville Railroad.	Hannibal & St. Joe Railroad.	Chicago, Burlington & Quincy Ry.	Ind., Cinn. & Lafayette Railroad.	St. Louis, Kansas City & Northern.
	Cents.	Cents.	Cents.	Cents.	Cents.	Cents.	Cents.	Cents.	Cents.	Cents.	Cents.	Cents.	Cents.	Cents.
For 25 miles..........	**12**	.20	18	16	16	.15	16	16	9	24	20	22	17	26
50 "	**20**	.28	24	26	22	.22	22	22	14	38	29	32	25	36
75 "	**24**	.38	28	34	26	.31	28	28	18	48	34	42	30	46
100 "	**28**	.48	36	48	32	.40	33	33	24	54	40	50	36	56
125 "	**32**	.56	42	58	36	.45	40	40	26	60	44	56	41	61
150 "	**36**	.68	46	66	40	.54	45	45	29	62	48	60	46	64
175 "	**40**	.76	54	72	44	.60	50	50	31	70	50	66	51	66
200 "	**44**	.80	60	72	50	.67	52	52	34	..	50	70	56	67
225 "	**45**	.88	..	72	54	.73	54	54	36	..	50	76	62	69
250 "	**46**	.92	..	72	60	.78	56	56	39	..	..	80	67	70
275 "	**47**	.98	..	..	66	.81	56	56	42	..	..	86	72	70
300 "	**48**	1.00	..	..	70	.84	56	56	44	..	..	90	..	70
325 "	**49**	1.04	..	..	76	.87	..	..	47	..	..	..	..	..
350 "	**50**	1.06	..	..	80	.90	..	..	49	..	..	..	..	..
375 "	**51**	1.08	..	..	84	.95	..	..	52	..	..	..	..	..
400 "	**52**	1.12	..	..	90	1.00	..	..	..	..	..	..	..	..

EXHIBIT "G."

Comparative Statement of Live Stock Rates.

Rates on Live Stock per Car Load.	**Potter Law Rates.**	N. Eng. Lines.		Trunk Lines.					Western and Southern Lines.					
		Boston & Albany.	Vermont Central.	Rome, Wat. & Ogd.	Phila. & Reading.	P., Ft. W. & C.	Michigan Central.	Atlantic & Great Western Rd.	Lou., Nash. & Gt. Southern Rd.	St. Louis, Kansas City & N. Rd.	Chicago, Bur. & Q.	Ind., Cinn. & Lafayette.	Hannibal & St. Joe Railroad.	Ohio & Miss. Rd.
For 25 miles......	**$10**	$16	$16	$16	$18	$15	$ 14	$ 9	$15	$23	$17	$15	$20	$ 15.00
50 "	**17**	24	21	27	28	25	18	14	29	33	27	23	28	20.50
75 "	**21**	28	28	32	36	37	25	20	35	39	37	29	33	24.50
100 "	**25**	36	34	39	40	45	30	24	45	44	47	34	39	28.75
125 "	**29**	42	40	46	44	48	34	26	58	45	53	39	44	32.50
150 "	**33**	46	44	50	48	54	36	29	65	48	57	45	49	34.75
175 "	**37**	54	50	..	52	60	38	31.50	80	50	63	50	54	38.00
200 "	**41**	60	57	..	..	64	40	34	..	53	67	58	55	.....
225 "	**45**	..	62	..	..	70	44	36	..	55	73	64	55	.....
250 "	**49**	..	68		..	74	50	39	..	58	75	70	.....	.....
275 "	**53**	..	72		..	78	..	42	..	58	78	75	..	.....
300 "	**57**	..	76	..	..	82	..	44	..	58	80	..	..	.....
325 "	**61**	..	80	..	..	86	..	47	..	..	..	..	..	.....
350 "	**65**	..	82	..	..	96	..	49	..	..	..	..	..	.....
375 "	**69**	..	84	..	..	100	..	51	..	..	..	..	..	.....
400 "	**73**	..	86	..	..	106	..	..	..	..	..	..	..	.....

EXHIBIT "H."

Comparative Rates on Agricultural Implements, Furniture and Wagons.

Rates on Agricultural Implements, Furniture and Wagons per Car.	Potter Law Rates.	N. England.		Trunk Lines.					Western and Southern Roads.				
		Vermont Central Road.	Boston & Albany Road.	Pitts., Ft. Wayne & Chicago Ry.	Lake Shore & M. Southern Ry.	Michigan Central Road.	Great Western Road.	Atlantic & Great Western Road.	Chicago, Burlington & Quincy Ry.	Indianapolis, Cincinnati & Lafayette Road.	St. Louis, Kansas Kansas City & N. Road.	Hamilton & St. Joe Road.	Louisville & Nashville Road.
For 25 miles	**$11.00**	$20.40	$14.00	$14.00	$15.00	$14.00	$17.00	$ 9.00	$22.00	$23.40	$24.00	$26.00	$15.00
" 50 "	**17.00**	28.80	19.20	19.00	20.00	22.00	26.00	14.00	34.00	30.60	34.00	36.00	30.00
" 75 "	**20.00**	36.00	24.00	28.00	25.00	24.00	32.00	20.00	44.00	34.20	43.00	46.00	37.00
" 100 "	**23.00**	48.00	28.80	37.00	28.00	32.00	37.00	24.00	54.00	39.60	48.00	53.00	44.00
" 125 "	**26.00**	55.20	32.00	41.00	32.00	34.00	42.00	26.00	60.00	46.80	52.00	58.00	55.00
" 150 "	**29.00**	60.00	39.60	48.00	36.00	42.00	49.00	29.50	64.00	54.00	55.00	63.00	60.00
" 175 "	**32.00**	69.60	45.60	54.00	38.00	44.00	54.00	31.50	70.00	61.20	57.00	68.00	70.00
" 200 "	**35.00**	74.40	50.40	60.00	43.00	44.00	60.00	34.00	74.00	66.60	60.00	70.00	.....
" 225 "	**38.00**	81.60	.....	65.00	48.00	46.00	64.00	36.00	80.00	72.00	62.00	70.00	.....
" 250 "	**41.00**	84.00	.....	68.00	53.00	50.00	66.00	39.00	84.00	81.00	65.00	.....	.....
" 275 "	**44.00**	87.60	.....	71.00	.....	.....	67.00	42.00	90.00	90.00	65.00	.....	.....
" 300 "	**47.00**	88.80	.....	74.00	.....	.....	67.00	44.00	94.00	.....	65.00	.....	.....
" 325 "	**50.00**	92.40	.....	76.00	.....	.....	.....	47.00	.....	.....	.....	.....	.....
" 350 "	**53.00**	93.60	.....	79.00	.....	.....	.....	49.00	.....	.....	.....	.....	.....
" 375 "	**56.00**	94.80	.....	83.00	.....	.....	.....	52.00	.....	.....	.....	.....	.....

EXHIBIT "I."

Comparative Rates on Salt, Cement, Lime, Etc.

Rates on Salt, Cement, Lime, Etc., Per Barrel.	Potter Law Rates.	New England.		Trunk Lines.						Western Lines.				
		Vermont Central Railroad.	Boston & Albany Railroad.	Pennsylvania Railroad.	Erie Railway.	Pittsburgh, Ft. Wayne & Chicago Railway.	Michigan Central Railroad.	Lake Shore & Mich. Southern Railroad.	Atlantic & Great Western Railway.	Chicago, Burlington & Quincy Railway.	Illinois Central Railroad.	Indianapolis, Cincinnati & Lafayette Railroad.	St. Louis, Kansas City & Northern Railroad.	Hannibal & St. Joe Railway.
	Cents.	Cents.	Cents.	Cents.	Cents.	Cents.	Cents.	Cents.	Cents.	Cents.	Cents.	Cents.	Cents.	Cents.
For 25 miles......	**15**	.23	21	.23	.24	.16	14	18	11	.36	28.00	20	30	22
" 50 "	**21**	.30	30	.30	.33	.24	18	23	20	.46	38.00	25	40	34
" 75 "	**24½**	.40	36	.35	.39	.45	24	29	25	.55	42.00	31	50	40
" 100 "	**28**	.48	42	.35	.48	.45	30	32	28	.60	44.80	36	60	50
" 125 "	**31½**	.57	54	.50	.54	.48	34	37	32	.66	48.00	41	66	57
" 150 "	**35**	.63	57	.56	.60	.57	36	41	37	.70	48.90	46	70	60
" 175 "	**38 ½**	.71	66	.63	.66	.63	38	47	41	.76	51.20	49	73	60
" 200 "	**42**	.77	72	.70	.75	.69	40	53	48	.80	53.20	51	75	60
" 225 "	**45½**	.88	....	.82	.81	.72	44	58	49	.86	55.20	55	78	60
" 250 "	**49**	.92	....	.89	.90	.78	48	61	54	.90	57.20	59	80	......
" 275 "	**52½**	1.00	....	1.08	.99	.84	50	......	58	.96	58.90	62	80	......
" 300 "	**55**	1.05	....	1.15	1.05	.93	......	......	61	1.00	60.50	......	80	......
" 325 "	**59½**	1.11	....	1.20	1.14	.99	......	......	65	......	......	......	......	......
" 350 "	**63**	1.13	....	1.20	1.20	1.05	......	......	66	......	......	......	......	......
" 375 "	**66½**	1.17	....	1.20	1.26	1.11	......	......	68	......	......	......	......	......
" 400	**70**	1.20	....	1.20	1.32	1.17	......	......	......	......	......	......	......	......

EXHIBIT "J."

Comparative Statement of Rates on Coal, Brick, Sand, Stone, Etc.

Rates on Coal, Brick, Sand, Stone, Etc., Per Car Load.	**Potter Law Rates.**	N.Eng. Lines.		Trunk Lines.							Western Lines.			
		Vermont Central Road.	Boston & Albany Road.	Pennsylvania Road.	Erie Railway.	Pittsburgh, Ft. Wayne & Chicago.	Michigan Central Road.	Lake Shore&Mich. Southern Ry.	Great Western of Canada.	Atlantic & Great Western Road.	Hannibal & St.Joe Road.	St. Louis, Kansas City & Northern Road.	Chicago, Burlington & Quincy Ry.	Indianapolis, Cincinnati & Lafayette Road.
For 25 miles	**$ 8.00**	$14.00	$11.40	$16.00	$16.00	$11.00	$10.00	$10.00	$11.00	$ 7.00	$15.00	$21.00	$17.00	$13.00
" 50 "	**14.00**	19.00	20.00	17.30	22.00	16.00	14.00	13.00	14.00	12.00	20.00	27.00	28.00	17.00
" 75 "	**16.00**	26.00	24.00	22.40	26.00	22.00	16 00	17.00	19.00	14.00	25.00	32.00	38.00	20.00
" 100 "	**19.00**	30.00	28.00	25.90	32.00	30.00	24.00	20.00	22.00	17.00	30.00	37.00	48.00	24.00
" 125 "	**21.50**	36.00	34.00	27.50	36.00	32.00	26.00	23.00	26.00	19.00	35.00	42.00	54.00	28.00
" 150 "	**24.00**	40.00	38.00	30.00	40.00	38.00	30.00	27.00	30.00	22.50	40.00	45.00	58.00	30.50
" 175 "	**26.50**	46.00	44.00	35.00	44.00	42.00	32.00	30.00	33.00	24.50	45.00	48.00	64.00	33.00
" 200 "	**29.00**	50.00	48.00	40.00	50.00	46.00	34.00	33.00	35.00	27.50	45.00	50.00	68.00	36.00
" 225 "	**31.50**	56.00	.....	41.50	54.00	48.00	34.00	34.00	38.00	29.50	45.00	52.00	74.00	41.00
" 250 "	**34.00**	60.00	.....	45.00	60.00	52.00	38.00	40.00	40.00	32.00	45.00	54.00	77.00	47.00
" 275 "	**36.00**	64.00	.....	49.50	66.00	56.00	40.00	.....	42.00	35.00	.....	54 00	80.00	56.00
" 300 "	**39.00**	68.00	.....	54.00	70.00	62.00	.....	.....	44.00	37.00	.....	54.00	82.00	.....
" 325 "	**41.50**	72.00	.....	72.00	76.00	66.00	.....	.....	.....	39.00	.....	.....	.....	.....
" 350 "	**44.00**	74.00	.....	72.00	80.00	70.00	.....	.....	.....	40.00	.....	.....	.....	.....
" 375 "	**46.50**	76.00	.....	72.00	84.00	74.00	.....	.....	.....	41.00	.....	.....	.....	.....
" 400 "	**49.00**	78.00	.....	72.00	90.00	78.00	.....	.....	.....	42.00	.....	.....	.....	.....

EXHIBIT "K."

Comparative Statement of Distance Tariff Rates on British Railways.

Rates on Flour per Barrel.	Potter Law Rates.	England.				Scotland.	Ireland.
		Midland Railway.	North Eastern Railway.	Great Eastern Railway.	London, Brighton and South Coast Ry.	Glasgow and South Western Railway.	Great Southern and Western Railway.
	Cents.	Cents.	Cents.	Cents.	Cents.	Cents.	Cents.
For 25 miles...........	12	12	12	10	8	12	10.00
" 50 "	20	20	20	18	15	22	18.00
" 75 "	24	27	27	23	22	30	20.00
" 100 "	28	36	36	30	30	40	24.75
" 125 "	32	45	45	37	37	50	31.25
" 160 "	86	54	54	44	44	60	37.00
" 175 "	40	63	63	52	52	70	44.00
" 200 "	44	72	72	60	60	80	50.00
Rates on Grain per 100 Pounds.							
	Cents.	Cents.	Cents.	Cents.	Cents.	Cents.	Cents.
For 25 miles...........	6	6	6	5	4.00	6	5.00
" 50 "	10	10	10	9	7.50	11	9.00
" 75 "	12	14	14	12	11.00	15	10.00
" 100 "	14	18	18	15	15.00	20	12.37
" 125 "	16	22	22	19	19.00	25	15.50
" 150 "	18	27	27	22	22.00	30	18.50
" 175 "	20	31	31	26	26.00	35	22.00
" 200 "	22	36	36	30	30.00	40	25.00

EXHIBIT "L."

Comparative Statement of Distance and Tariff Rates on British Railways.

Rates on Salt and Cement, per Bbl.	Potter Law Rates.	England.			Ireland.		Scotland.
		Midland Ry.	North Eastern Ry.	Great Eastern	Midland Great Western Ry.	Great Southern and Western Ry.	Glasgow and South Western Ry.
	Cents.	Cents.	Cents.	Cents.	Cents.	Cents.	Cents.
For 25 miles	15	.16	14	11	11	14	.14
" 50 "	21	.28	23	21	22	22	.27
" 75 "	24½	.42	26	24	32	26	.42
" 100 "	28	.56	35	32	43	36	.56
" 125 "	31½	.70	44	41	53	46	.70
" 150 "	35	.84	53	48	63	56	.84
" 200 "	38½	1.00	61	55	74	61	1.00
" 250 "	32	1.12	70	63	82	70	1.12
Rates on Live Stock, per Car.							
For 50 miles	$17	$15	$13	$15	$15		$27
" 75 "	21	22	19	22	22		37
" 100 "	25	30	25	30	30		49
" 125 "	29	37	32	37	37		62
" 150 "	33	45	38	45	45		74
" 175 "	37	52	44	52	52		86
" 200 "	41	60	50	60	60		98

EXHIBIT "M."

Comparative Statement of Distance Tariff Rates on English Railways.

Rates on Brick and Stone Per Car Load.	Potter Law Rates.	London and Northwestern Railway.	Lancashire and Yorkshire Railway.	Great Northern Railway.	Midland Railway.	North Eastern Railway.	London and South Western Railway.
For 25 miles	**$8.00**	$ 9.00	$10.12	$ 7.50	$ 6.20	$10.00	$ 7.50
" 50 "	**14.00**	15.00	16.20	12.50	10.00	15.00	15.00
" 75 "	**16.50**	18.00	18.50	13.75	15.00	18.75	18.75
" 100 "	**19.00**	22.00	24.00	18.00	20.00	24.75	24.75
" 125 "	**21.50**	25.25	27.00	21.00	24.75	31.00	31.00
" 150 "	**24.00**	29.00	33.40	24.75	30.00	37.00	37.00

Comparative Distance Tariff Rates on Agricultural Implements and Wagons.

	Potter Law Rates.	On All English Roads
For 25 miles	**$11.00**	$16.00*
" 50 "	**17.00**	24.00
" 75 "	**20.00**	33.75
" 100 "	**23.00**	43.75
" 125 "	**26.00**	53.75
" 150 "	**29.00**	63.75

* See Clearing House Classification A. S., p. 15, App. to Evidence.

EXHIBIT "N."

Results of Operations on British Railways for the year 1872.

	Number of miles operated.	Gross Receipts from Passengers. Total.	Passengers. Proportion to total Receipts	Freight. Total.	Freight. Proportion to total Receipts	Traffic. Total.	Traffic. Per Mile.	All Sources. Total.	Expenses. Total.	Expenses. Proportion to Receipts.
For 1871..........	15,376	£20,622,580	42.18	£26,484,978	54.17	£47,107,558	£3,064	£48,892,780	£23,152,860	47
" 1872..........	15,814	22,287,555	41.87	29,016,559	54.50	51,304,114	3,244	53,235,510	26,293,304	49

	Number of Miles Operated.	Gross Receipts—Passenger. From First Class.	From Second Class.	From Third Class (including Parliamentary Trains.)	From Miscellan. Sources.	From All Sources.	Gross Receipts—Freight. From Freight.	From Miscellan. Sources.	From All Sources.	Per cent. of Pass. to total earnings.
England & Wales,.	11,136	£3,654,754	£3,669,736	£8,681,494	£2,865,819	£18,876,764	£24,499,414	£1,662,977	£45,039,155	41
Scotland..........	2,587	397,226	228,531	1,106,163	355,875	2,087,795	3,454,975	232,320	5,775,090	34
Ireland...........	2,091	267,205	299,934	531,104	224,285	1,322,996	1,062,170	36,099	2,421,265	54

EXHIBIT "O."

Passenger Rates per Mile on English, Scotch and Irish Railroads.

Name of Railroad.	By Express Trains.		By Ordinary Trains.			Scotland and Ireland.	By Ordinary Trains.		
	1st Class.	2d Class.	1st Class.	2d Class.	3d Class.		1st Class.	2d Class.	3d Class.
	Cents.	Cents.	Cents.	Cents.	Cents.		Cents.	Cents.	Cents.
London, Chatham & Dover..	6.10	4.17	5.62	3.84	2	Highland..........	4	3	2
South Eastern...........	5½	4.16	5	3.60	1.94	Glasgow & So. West'n.	4	2	2
North London...........	5	4	6	4	2	——			
London & North Western..	....	....	4	3	2				
Great Northern..........	....	....	12	8	2	Dubl. Wickl. & Wexf.	4.62	3.36	2
Furness	....	....	5	4	3	Ulster	5.35	2½	2
North Eastern...........	....	....	5	4	3	Dublin & Belfast Junc.	5¼	2.60	2

EXHIBIT "P."

Maximum Passenger Rates and Revenue from Passengers on Ohio Roads During 1873.

NAME OF RAILROAD.	For shortest distance.	For more than 8 and less than 30 miles.	For more than 30 and less than 100 miles.	Highest Rate for whole length of Road.	Lowest Rate for through Passengers.	Per centage of Passenger earnings to Freight.	Earnings from Passengers per mile.	Earnings from through Passengers.	Earnings from local Passengers.
	Cents.	Cents.	Cents.	Cents	Cents.				
Chicago, Mil. & St. Paul Ry...	**3**	**3**	**3**	**3**		**28**	**$1,327.51**	**$309,453.80**	**$1,547,742.63**
Atlantic & Gt. Western Rd......	5	4	3.50	3	2.16	42	1,702.93	339,105.02	691,169.67
Cincinnati, Ham. & Dayton Rd..	10	4	3	2.83	2.50	54	5,362.10	43,356.80	273,010.33
Marietta & Cincinnati Rd......	10	3.50	3.50	3.40	3	32	1,776.40	155,202.95	345,202.95
Cleveland & Pittsburgh Rd......	5	3.75	3.50	3.50	1.37	18	2,919.54	196,602.29	460,294.77
Pittsburgh, Ft. Wayne & Cin. Ry	5	3.50	3.50	3.50	2	35	5,011.53	1,077,675.82	1,443,124.49
Lake Shore & Mich. Southern Ry.	5	4	3.50	3.20	3.33	30	3,959.90	945.072.65	3,624,657.09
Central Ohio................	13.50	4.17	3.50	3.33	2	37	1,979.31	....	....
Cincinnati & Sandusky Ry.....	8.57	4	4	3.50	3	46	1,106.88	49,556.27	160,751.08
Cleve., Col., & Ind. Ry.........	3.50	3.50	3.50	3.50	2	22	2,110.03	468,960.78	356,064.32
Cincinnati & Musk. Valley Rd..	7.50	3.50	3.50	3.50	2.35	44	872.85	....	....
Chicago & North Western Ry..	**3**	**3**	**3**	**3**	....	**33**	**2,301.42**	**905,461.66**	**2,521,362.69**

EXHIBIT "Q."

Statement of Cost per mile and Dividends paid on the following named Roads, by States.

New York.	Cost Per Mile.	Stock and Debt Per Mile.	Rate of Dividends.	Pennsylvania.	Cost Per Mile.	Rate of Dividend On Preferred Stock.	Rate of Dividend On Common Stock.
Albany & Susquehanna	$51,542.08	$49,694.00	7	Alleghany Valley	$93,426.00	......	......
Buffalo, New York & Phila.	45,041.00	45,014.55	......	Philadelphia & Erie	82.384.19	......	......
Erie	124,335.00	138,937.54	1¾	Pennsylvania	136,037.37	......	10
Harlem	97,249.00	94.870.17	8	Delaware, Lackawana & Western	108,827.45	......	10
Rensselaer & Saratoga	49,659.00	46,909.00	8	Northern Central	111,810.75	......	6
NewYorkCen. & Hudson River	98,483,00	146,839.48	8	Pittsburgh & Connellsville	87,545.46	......	......
New York, Boston & Montreal,	82,861.00	89,614.35	......	Phila , Wilmington & Baltimore,	124,365.00	......	10
New York & Oswego Midland	62,378.00	61,158.98	......	Delaware & Hudson	101,691.68	......	......
Average	76,493.51	84,129.80	......	Average	105,761.10	......	......
New England.				**Ohio.**			
Boston & Albany	$87,636.70	$105,048.10	10	Ohio & Mississippi	89,844.00	7	......
Boston, Hartford & Erie	83,780.84	86,206.89	......	Cincinnati, Hamilton & Dayton	93,932.00	......	8
Boston & Lowell	65,975.82	110,832.30	8	Cleveland & Pittsburg	78,634.00	......	7
Boston & Maine	71,108.39	78,981.44	8	Pittsburgh, Ft. Wayne & Chicago	58,013 00	7	7
Eastern	54,557.59	93,171.39	6	Pittsburgh, Cinn. & St. Louis	95,241.00	......	......
Pittsburg	40,186.55	42,961.37	8	Toledo, Wabash & Western	55,905.00	7	......
Old Colony	36,673.52	39,789.58	7	Dayton & Michigan	48,469.00	8	3⅓
Boston & Providence	63,118,64	81,042.32	10	Cleveland,Columbus,Cinn.&Ind.	42,769.00	......	7
Average	71,673.52	85,900,66	......	Average	70,350.87	......	......

EXHIBIT "R."

Results of Operations on the Four Largest English Railways for the year 1872.

Name of Railroad.	Number of miles operated.	Gross Receipts — From Passengers. From 1st class.	From 2d class.	From 3d class.	From all sources.	Freight. From Freight.	Total. From all sources.	Earnings per Mile. Gross.	Net.	Average Cost of Road per Mile.	Proportion of Working Expenses to Receipts.
		£	£	£	£	£	£	£	£	£	
Great Western	1402	430,045	512,099	988,824	2,243,700	2,668,466	4,984,052	3,554	1,896	34,361	47
Midland	1024	205,740	227,935	835,369	1,516,977	3,556,447	5,134,213	5,013	2,666	41,548	47
London & North Western	1539	257,412	620,620	1,412,031	3,364,066	4,647,029	8,119,832	5,276	2,774	39,413	47
North Eastern	1337	216,024	209,511	772,545	1,437,177	3,888,505	5,434,968	4,065	2,100	33,461	48

EXHIBIT "S."

Comparative Statement of Number of Passengers carried on the Roads named.

NAME OF ROAD.	Length of Road.	Number of Passengers carried.	Number of Passengers carried per mile of road.	NAME OF ROAD.	Length of Road.	Number of Passengers carried.	Number of Passengers carried per mile of road.
Chicago, Milwaukee & St. Paul,	**1399**	**967,754**	**692**	**Chicago & Northwestern,**	**1489**	**2,823,889**	**1,869**
Boston & Albany,	282	5,757,624	20,417	Boston & Providence,	66	3,741,530	56,690
Boston & Lowell,	80	2,086,779	26,085	Boston & Maine,	164	5,008,074	30,537
Connecticut River,	56	1,124,300	20,077	Eastern,	364	5,696,351	21,577
Old Colony,	257	4,256,840	16,563	Providence & Worcester,	60	1,785,067	29,577
New York & New Haven,	153	3,892,674	25,542	NewYorkCent'l & Hudson River.	858	7,630,741	8,893
New Jersey Central	292	4,401,326	15,073	United Railroads of New Jersey,	278	8,003,043	28,790
Morris & Essex,	137	2,500,000	18,249	Long Island,	158	1,000,000	6,330
Alleghany Valley,	262	861,293	3,288	Lehigh Valley,	230	1,096,820	4,768
Northern Central,	142	1,180,322	8,312	Pennsylvania,	828	5,879,684	7,101
Phila., Wilm. & Baltimore,	105	2,331,722	12,207	Pittsburgh & Connellsville,	169	859,533	5,086
Cincinnati, Hamilton & Dayton,	59	731,228	12,392	Little Miami,	196	723,785	3,693
Michigan Central,	285	877,446	3,078	Pittsburg, Ft. Wayne & Chicago,	500	2,107,268	4,215
Lake Shore & Mich. Southern,	1180	2,845,163	2,411	Jefferson, Mad. & Indianapolis,	226	658,928	2,915

www.ingramcontent.com/pod-product-compliance
Lightning Source LLC
Chambersburg PA
CBHW032117080426
42733CB00008B/965
9783744696838